DISCOVERERS

Series Editor: Bradford Chambers

A Who · When · Where Book

OF AMERICA

PRIMITIVE MAN TO SPANISH CONQUERORS

Written by Felix Sutton

Pictures by Leonard Vosburgh

Consultant and Co-Author
V. Phillips Weaver, Ed. D.
Assistant Professor of Education, University of Maryland

Grosset & Dunlap   New York

Introduction

This book has been written to bring pleasure to its readers. The story of the discovery of America is interesting and exciting to read, of course. But only part of it tells of heroes, of daring, of fame, and of riches. The adventures of those who left their homelands to explore new lands often included hardship and disappointment. It takes courage today to travel into outer space; the early explorers knew even less about the newly found lands across the sea.

Discoverers of America is one of a series of books which has special value as a supplementary reader in the Social Studies. Developed under the guidance of an Advisory Committee* of recognized authorities in this field drawn from all parts of the U.S.A., each book has been written by a popular author in consultation with a qualified expert in the subject area.

Special attention is called to the cover. An exceptional effect has been achieved by photographing figures and objects of paper sculpture. Every paper figure and object has been made three-dimensional through the skill of its creator, Erica Egan.

*ADVISORY COMMITTEE

Miss Helen Fairweather
Elementary School Teacher
Decatur, Illinois Public Schools

Dr. Lloyd L. Smith
Associate Professor of Education
University of Iowa

Dr. J. D. McAulay
Associate Professor of Education
Pennsylvania State University

Dr. Thomas D. Horn
Chairman, Department Curriculum
    and Instruction
University of Texas

Dr. John Jarolimek
Associate Professor of Education
University of Washington

Library of Congress Catalog Card Number: 65-13780

Book designed by Leslie B. Tanner

Contents

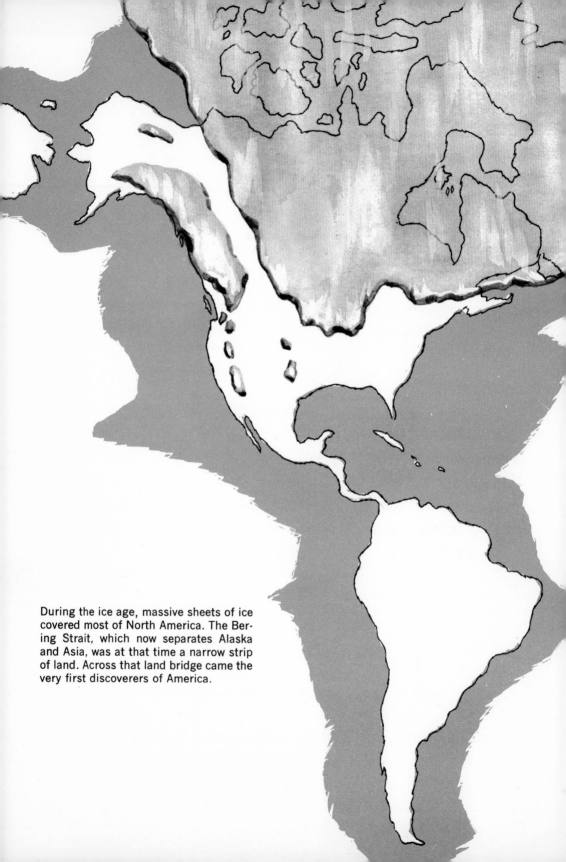

During the ice age, massive sheets of ice covered most of North America. The Bering Strait, which now separates Alaska and Asia, was at that time a narrow strip of land. Across that land bridge came the very first discoverers of America.

CHAPTER 1

THE FIRST DISCOVERERS

EVERYBODY KNOWS that Christopher Columbus discovered America. But he was by no means the first man to do so. He was simply the first to tell the rest of the world about it. The original discoverers of America beat Columbus by about 20,000 years.

At that time, more than 200 centuries ago, the landscape of what we now call the United States looked much the same as it does today. There were the same mountains towering into the sky; the same rolling prairies; the same dense forests of pine and hardwood; the same sparkling lakes and rivers. The Rockies were just as high; the mighty Mississippi just as wide; the Grand Canyon just as awe-inspiring — if there had been any human eyes to see it.

WHAT WAS AMERICA LIKE IN THE ICE AGE?

But in that far-distant day, there was not a single human being in all the broad expanse of either North or South America. The wild beasts ruled supreme, unmolested except by each other.

9

If you could ride a magic carpet back through time and see the land as it was then, you would recognize all but a few of the animals that roamed the vast woodlands and grazed on the grassy plains. There were deer, bears, antelope, buffaloes, wolves, rabbits, and squirrels. There were huge herds of shaggy wild horses. In addition, there were strange creatures that we do not usually associate with America of species that have long since disappeared — "giraffe camels" 18 feet tall; huge, shaggy elephant-like beasts with great incurving tusks; and large, ferocious saber-toothed cats.

HOW WAS ALASKA LINKED WITH ASIA?

To the north, however, things were different. This was the tag-end of the Pleistocene Period, more commonly called the ice age, and almost all of what is now Canada and Alaska was covered by a tremendous glacier of solid ice that, in places, was as much as 10,000 feet thick. One result of this great accumulation of frozen water was to lower the level of the seas, so that a narrow isthmus of land connected Alaska and Asia where Bering Strait now separates them.

Stone-tipped spear and hatchet used by the first Americans.

Thus Nature, in that time long ago, set the scene for man's first discovery of a great New World.

Across the land bridge from Asia to Alaska wandered the nomadic hunters. We don't know just when. They were a Mongoloid people, of the same race as the Chinese, Japanese, and other Eastern peoples. They had straight black hair and coppery or brownish skins. Their clothes were cut crudely from skins and furs, and they carried stone hatchets and stone-tipped spears. Small, scraggly hunting dogs, little more than half-tamed wolves, tagged along at their heels.

Intent on tracking down animals for food, this group of men, women, and children had no idea that they were the first people to set foot on a new and undiscovered continent. And even if they had, it would have meant nothing to them. The farther they moved south, the more pleasant became the climate and the more plentiful the game. So, as one year passed slowly into another, they and their descendants kept going deeper and deeper into a wonderful country that was beautiful as well as bountiful.

"Giraffe camels," mammoth elephant-like beasts, and large saber-toothed cats roamed America before nomad hunters wandered across the land bridge from Asia.

The Indians hunted wild game. Later, they grew food by scratching the earth with sticks and planting seeds.

Small bands of hunters continued to cross the land bridge from Asia until most of it disappeared. They, too, moved southward, following the weather and the game. Down through Alaska and Canada, they came — a few miles each year or each hundred years — into the mountains and plains of what is now the western United States. From there, some wandered eastward into the Great Lakes country, and beyond it, to the Atlantic Coast. Others kept on going south into Mexico and Central America, and then, across the narrow neck of Panama and over the Equator into Peru, Brazil, and Chile. Some of them even got as far south as Tierra del Fuego, the extreme tip of South America, on the edge of the Antarctic Circle.

Wherever they went in their wanderings, a few stayed behind and settled down. After a few thousand years, the whole of the New World was populated by the descendants of the vagrant hunters who had crossed over from Asia so long before.

Meanwhile, the ice age glacier had melted and the seas filled up again. The Siberia-Alaska land bridge

12

Indians made moccasins and tents from animal skins. From the tendons, they made bow-strings and fishing lines. ▶

by now had disappeared completely, and this new grouping of people was isolated from the rest of mankind. We call them the Indians — the first Americans.

These original discoverers of America adjusted their lives and their mode of living to the parts of the country in which they finally settled down. They were hunters, stalking their game and killing it with spears and clubs. They were able to throw their spears for short distances by means of crude slings. From this primitive device, they eventually developed the bow and arrow.

They made clothing, moccasins, and tents from animal skins. From the tendons, they fashioned bowstrings, fishing lines, and thread for sewing. They trapped fish in nets woven from roots or willow branches, and caught them on hooks carved from pieces of bone. They lived on a diet of meat and fish, varied with wild fruits and vegetables.

HOW DID THE INDIANS BECOME FARMERS?

Then, in time, the Indians gradually became farmers as well as hunters — particularly those in the East and South, where the soil was rich and fertile. We can imagine that farming began when the Indians found certain plants that especially pleased them. They probably encouraged these plants by weeding around them and loosening the soil to help them grow. This naturally would lead to the replanting of the most choice seeds. And so, in a long, drawn-out process of evolution, the Indians began cultivating domesticated crops.

In this manner, the Indians developed a great many vegetables that were unknown in Europe before the time of Columbus, but which are common to our modern dinner tables: corn, beans, squash, pumpkins, and potatoes. They also grew the first tobacco, which they smoked in clay pipes called calumets.

Indians invented snowshoes for winter travel and pulled loads on birchbark sleds. In the summer, rivers were their principal roadways.

Lodge Sign

Head of Horse

The farming methods of the American Indians were primitive and crude. They had no way to clear or plow fields, so they planted their crops in natural clearings in the forest or in places that had been burned out by lightning fires. They simply scratched the ground with pointed sticks, and sowed the seed in crooked rows that zigzagged crazily around the charred stumps.

Farm work was done by the women and children. The men were hunters and warriors, and they considered labor in the fields beneath their dignity.

Sun Sign

Rain Sign

When Columbus discovered America, there were about one million Indians scattered sparsely throughout the length and breadth of what is now the United States. They were divided into several hundred tribes, and they spoke just about as many different languages and dialects. It was not unusual for a tribe living in one

valley to be ignorant of the speech of a tribe that lived in another valley only a few miles away.

To an extent, the Indians overcame this barrier to communication by developing a sign language of gestures with arm, hands, and fingers that conveyed simple meanings. But except for war parties, Indians seldom ventured far from their own hunting grounds.

Many Indian words have become a living part of our American language. Usually, they are the names of places, lakes, and rivers like Mississippi, Tennessee, Ohio, Erie, Iowa, Kansas, Kentucky, Dakota, Oklahoma, Texas, Connecticut, Massachusetts, Miami, Wichita, Chicago. Others — skunk, raccoon, hickory, succotash,

15

squash, woodchuck, moose, Yankee — survive as nouns that are familiar to us all.

In the Indians' day, the country that is now the eastern United States was a vast, unending forest, broken up only by rivers that meandered between the hills. Aside from the woodland trails, these rivers were the Indians' principal roadways. They traveled along them in canoes made of birchbark or hollowed-out logs. In the wintertime, they made birchbark sleds for pulling loads over the ice and snow. They invented snowshoes for walking on top of the deep drifts. (It is interesting that our modern snowshoes have changed very little from the original Indian design.)

Although most of the eastern Indians were woodsmen, wandering ceaselessly through the forests in pursuit of game, many others lived in large towns. These Indian towns consisted of perhaps a hundred or more houses that were made of birchbark or deer skins stretched over a framework of sticks. The Iroquois lived in long, rectangular bark houses called long houses. Several families shared these homes. As a defense against raids

Indians of the South-west built cities on the sides of steep cliffs.

by enemy tribes, some towns were surrounded by high fences, or palisades, of sharply pointed logs. Outside the palisades were vegetable gardens, cornfields, and tobacco patches.

The tribes of the Southwest — in what is now New Mexico, Arizona, southern Utah, and northern Mexico — also developed a "town society." They were the Cliff Dwellers. They built cities of stone that clung like eagles' nests to the sides of the sheer canyon walls. On the mesas above their cliff-cities were the farms where they raised corn and beans, and the fields on which they pastured their flocks of goats and turkeys.

Unlike most American Indians, who lived in makeshift wigwams or tepees, the Cliff Dwellers built permanent "apartment houses" of stone three or four stories high, some with as many as 200 rooms. Steps chopped out of the cliff walls connected the various levels of the city, and led up to the fields on the mesa above.

The Plains Indians lived in tepees which they made from buffalo hides.

On the treeless prairies northeast of the Cliff Dwellers, between the Mississippi River and the Rocky Mountains, lived the tribes that we call the Plains Indians. They established no permanent homes at all, but moved their tepee villages from place to place to follow the buffalo herds.

The Plains Indians developed little agriculture. Their lives revolved around the buffalo, which, in those times, numbered in the tens of millions. Aside from the few wild roots and berries they picked, and the occasional dish of stewed dog they ate on special occasions, the Plains Indians' main food was buffalo meat. Their clothes and the covering for their tepees were made from buffalo hide, and their few primitive tools were made from its bones. They even made their fires from dried buffalo droppings.

The Plains tribes roamed all over the West, never settling down for more than a few weeks or a few months in any one place. When the buffalo moved on to new grass, the Indians folded up their tepees and followed them.

These, then, were the people who inhabited America before the coming of the white men. And no one in all the rest of the world knew that they, or the great land in which they lived, even existed.

Buffalo meat — herds in the millions roamed the West — was the chief food of the Plains Indians.

CHAPTER 2

SEA ROVERS

THE FIRST Europeans to set foot in the New World were bands of wild and woolly sea rovers. They were vikings. Originally, they had come from Sweden, Denmark, and Norway, and had been pirates by profession. They sailed the seas in great ships built in the shape of dragons, looting the coastal towns of Germany, France, England, Ireland, Italy, and Spain. The mere sight of an approaching viking dragon-ship, with its big, brightly-colored sail and its rows of long oars on either side, was enough to make the terrified townspeople run for the shelter of the forests. The vikings then sacked the deserted town, and usually burned what was left of it.

WHAT ISLAND DID THE VIKINGS DISCOVER?

The open sea was no fearsome barrier to the vikings, as it was to other Europeans. At a time when almost all sailors were afraid to venture beyond the sight of land, these Norsemen, guided only by the stars, struck out boldly across the unknown oceans. They established colonies in Ireland and on islands north of

19

Scotland. Some of them sailed as far south as the Mediterranean Sea, and through it to Constantinople, where they hired out as professional soldiers in the army of the Byzantine emperor.

But most of the vikings' explorations were westward. In A.D. 874, they discovered Iceland, and there, established a permanent colony.

In spite of the island's forbidding name, parts of Iceland that lie near the sea enjoy a relatively mild and hospitable climate. The grasslands were lush and rich, and the flocks of sheep and cattle that the vikings had brought with them flourished.

The original settlers prospered; more came after them, until, in a few years, the population of Iceland grew to more than 50,000 people. As time went by, the former pirates became law-abiding farmers. They created one of the world's first true democratic forms of government in 930. They developed a rich and extensive literature; it is from their poems and stories, called sagas, that we can follow the course of their history.

Viking shield

Iron axe used by vikings

The vikings were the first Europeans to discover America. Some scientists believe they landed in New England around the year 1000.

WHO WAS ERIC THE RED?

About a hundred years after the first Icelandic settlement, a man named Eric the Red because of the fiery color of his hair and beard set out in a dragon-ship to explore even farther west. The land that he found was locked in the grip of a vast glacier, as most of it still is today, except for one small area which was a grassy plain. Here, Eric founded a settlement, and then went back to Iceland to induce people to come and live in it. In order to make the place sound attractive, he named it Greenland.

Then, around the year 1000, Eric's son, Leif Ericson, sometimes called "Leif the Lucky," set sail from Greenland on another voyage of exploration. He, too, went westward. In due time, he came to a vast land of mountains and endless forests. Because grapevines grew in wild profusion among the trees, he called the new country "Vinland." From Leif's descriptions of the landscape, vegetation, and weather, some scientists believe that it was the coast of what is now New England.

Drinking mug

Viking dish

When he returned to Greenland, Leif's story created a great deal of excitement. In the years that followed, many other viking adventurers visited Vinland and explored it. On one voyage, a certain captain named Thorfinn Karlselfni, took his wife with him. During the year or so that the expedition stayed in Vinland, Thorfinn's wife bore him a son, Snorro. He, according to Icelandic legend, had the honor of being the first white child born in America.

After many fierce battles with the Indians, the vikings were driven out of Vinland.

Until recently, archaeologists had little proof that the vikings did actually visit America. But late in 1963, the remains of a small viking town were discovered near the fishing village of L'Anse aux Meadows, in Newfoundland. Traces of nine structures and a primitive smithy were excavated. One house had five rooms and a great hall, built in the viking style. Since radioactive dating methods indicate that the site was occupied about the year 1000, some authorities believe that this settlement may have been established by Leif Ericson either before or after he had sailed on southward to Vinland.

Additional evidence that the vikings came here consist of inscriptions carved in stones they often left behind them as they went from place to place. A number of these stones — they are called "rune stones" — have been found on Cape Cod and other places along the Massachusetts and Rhode Island shores.

One such viking stone was found as far west as Minnesota, beyond the Great Lakes. If this stone is genuine and not a hoax, as some historians have suggested, it would indicate that a party of Norsemen had plunged into the towering forest and crossed half the continent. The viking legends do not mention any such deep penetration of Vinland, so it is likely that these daring explorers were killed by Indians before they could find their way back to the coast.

In the beginning, the Indians — or "Skraelings," as the vikings called them — were friendly to the fierce-looking bearded strangers who had appeared out of the sea mists in their weird dragon-ships. They were glad to trade valuable furs for pieces of cloth and metal ornaments, the likes of which they had never seen before. Then, in time, arguments arose and fights broke out. After the first one, in which many of Thorfinn's company were killed, most of the Indians were the vikings' sworn enemies.

Viking dragon-ship

Thriving settlement in Greenland was founded by Eric the Red around the year 975.

The vikings fought with heavy swords and axes made of iron. The Indians used arrows, which they shot from behind the protection of trees, just as they did when tribe was fighting tribe. This kind of warfare was more than the vikings could cope with. At last, the fearsome Norse warriors had met their match.

DID THE VIKINGS COLONIZE VINLAND?

Even so, viking expeditions to Vinland continued. Some came to cut timber, for timber trees were non-existent in Greenland and Iceland. Others may have come to collect the abundant grapes for wine-making. After the vikings were converted to Christianity, Vinland was included in the Greenland bishopric. In 1121, a bishop sailed west to visit these remote parts of his

24

Icelandic sagas of daring viking explorations were narrated around campfires during long winter nights. ▶

diocese, but he was never heard of again. It is not known whether his ship was lost in a storm at sea, or whether he and his party were set upon and killed by the Skraelings. Most of the expeditions, however, came for adventure and exploration.

After the first short-lived attempt by Thorfinn, the vikings never tried to colonize Vinland. Gradually, the westward voyages died out, and the great land that lay beyond the setting sun was forgotten except in the sagas. In time, too, the Greenland colony was abandoned, and there were no Europeans left west of Iceland.

WHY WERE THEIR DISCOVERIES NOT KNOWN?

You may wonder why the vikings did not spread the news of their discovery of a vast western land

throughout Europe. In the first place, although they were the greatest seamen of their time, they had no true knowledge of world geography. As far as they were concerned, Greenland and Vinland were simply island extensions of Europe, as was Iceland.

Secondly, they told their stories only in their sagas, and these were not translated into any language that other Europeans could understand until more than 700 years after Leif Ericson's historic voyage. As time went by even the Norsemen themselves, save for a few scholars, forgot the sagas.

So, America continued to be what one historian has called the "biggest secret" in the world. At the time of Columbus, not even the most learned scientists and geographers in Europe had any idea that it existed.

It was not until Columbus tried to find a short-cut to the fabulous Indies, with his revolutionary idea of sailing west instead of east, that the presence on the globe of a New World was revealed.

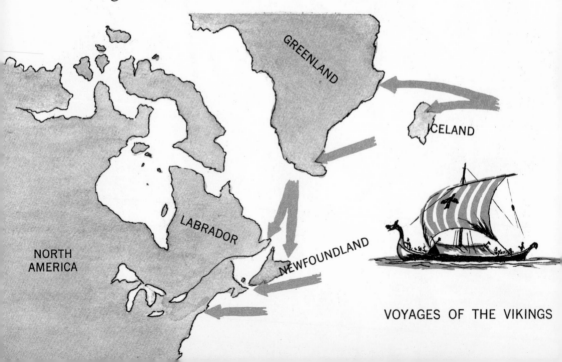

VOYAGES OF THE VIKINGS

CHAPTER 3

RICHES OF THE EAST

IN THE year 1271, two wealthy Italian brothers, Nicolò and Maffeo Polo, set out on the long journey to fabled Cathay, the land we now call China. With them went Nicolò's 17-year-old son, Marco.

At that time, virtually nothing was known in Europe about Cathay except for the fact that it existed. Yet wonderful tales were told about the wealth of its people — their clothes of richest silk, the priceless jewels they wore, the golden roofs of their palaces and temples, the exotic spices with which they flavored their food. The Polos, merchants, determined to bring back some of these treasures to sell in Italy.

HOW DID MARCO POLO REACH CHINA?

They traveled by boat across the Mediterranean to Palestine, and then by donkey through Persia, Afghanistan, and India, and across the vast Gobi Desert in Mongolia. At last, after three and a half years, they reached the capital city of the great Kublai Khan, ruler of almost all the Orient. The Emperor welcomed them, showered them with riches, and took them into his service as advisors.

As one of the Khan's emissaries, Marco Polo journeyed into nearly every part of the vast empire. On these trips, he discovered for himself that the fabulous stories of the wealth of the East were true. More important, he took copious notes wherever he went.

When the Polos finally returned to Venice, more than 20 years after they had departed, they brought with them a huge fortune in silks, spices, and precious gems. But their adventures might have been quickly forgotten if Marco had not been taken prisoner, a few years later, in a war between the rival city-states of Venice and Genoa. Sitting alone in his cell with nothing to do, he remembered his travel notes. He sent for

Marco Polo's journey to Cathay took 3½ years. He traversed the Gobi Desert, crossed the Tibetan mountains, and arrived in what is now Peking.

Kublai Khan showered Marco Polo with riches.

them and wrote the now-classic *Book of Marvels*, a book that was to play an important part in changing the history of the world.

The book was widely read, and its remarkable detail sent the merchants of Italy on a wild scramble to establish regular trade with Cathay and other Oriental lands. As a result, for the next century and a half, the riches of the East were transported to Europe by ship and camel caravan over the long and arduous route that Marco Polo had pioneered.

WAS THERE AN ALL-SEA ROUTE TO CATHAY?

Then in 1453, the Turks, who had long been at war with the Christian nations, bottled up the land routes. The European traders began desperately seeking for an all-sea route to Cathay, the Spice Islands, and "Cipangu," the ancient name for Japan.

The best geographers and map-makers of the time went to work on the problem. They believed that there were two possible ways to get from Europe to the Orient by sea. One was to sail around Africa and on through the Indian Ocean. But no one could be certain that there was an open passage south of the African continent, and no sailors had ever made an attempt to find out. (Indeed, it was not until 1497, five years after

29

Columbus' first voyage to America, that the Portuguese navigator, Vasco da Gama, rounded the Cape of Good Hope and made a landing in India.)

The second route that the map-makers suggested was even more risky and fantastic. This was to sail due west across the unknown and fearsome Sea of Darkness, which we know as the Atlantic Ocean.

Since the days of ancient Greece, a few scholars had known that the earth was round like a ball, and not a flat and isolated island that floated in a mysterious sea. But they thought that it was much smaller than it actually is, and that nothing but water separated Europe from Cathay. They never dreamed that two great continents were in the way, and that beyond them lay still another ocean, twice as large as the Atlantic.

The westward route was so frightening, and so fraught with hidden danger, that not even the most daring sea captain wanted to test the theories of the map-makers. Then, a determined man named Christopher Columbus turned up in Portugal.

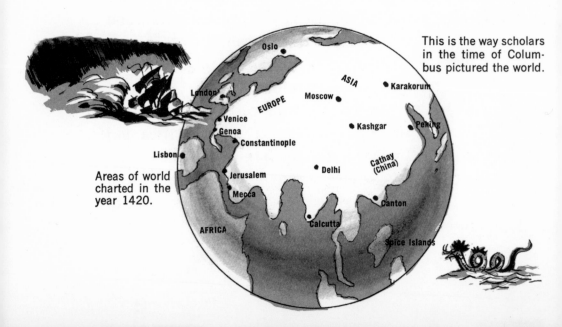

This is the way scholars in the time of Columbus pictured the world.

Areas of world charted in the year 1420.

Oslo

ASIA • Karakorum

London

EUROPE Moscow

Venice
Genoa
Constantinople • Kashgar Peking

Lisbon

Jerusalem • Delhi Cathay (China)

Mecca

Canton

AFRICA Calcutta

Spice Islands

CHAPTER 4

ADMIRAL OF THE OCEAN SEA

CHRISTOPHER COLUMBUS was born in Genoa, Italy, sometime around the year 1450. The old records do not show his exact birth date, and Columbus himself was inconsistent when he wrote about it in later years. He was the son of a wool-weaver.

Unlike most boys of that day and time who followed the professions of their fathers, young Christopher wanted nothing to do with the weaver's trade. He was in love with the sea. He spent most of his time strolling along the docks, talking to sailors and watching the cargo ships sail away from Genoa bound for faraway places. When he wasn't at the waterfront, he was studying Latin and poring over books of geography, astronomy, and navigation.

WHAT DID COLUMBUS HOPE TO ACCOMPLISH?

At the age of 14, Columbus went to sea for the first time. And in the years that followed he sailed all through the Mediterranean, down the coast of Africa as far as ships dared to go, and northward to England

31

Columbus wrote Paul the Physicist for advice on voyage.

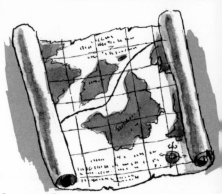

Chart of the Sea of Darkness

and Iceland. Between voyages he made maps, and soon became a skilled cartographer.

As he studied, his great dream began to take form. He had read Marco Polo's book about the wealth of the Orient; and he knew that it had taken that traveler more than three years to get there. Since, like other good map-makers, he knew that the world was round, he determined to take the short cut westward across the Atlantic.

In the city of Florence lived Paolo Toscanelli, known as Paul the Physicist, generally considered to be the foremost geographer in the world. Columbus wrote him a letter asking his opinion about such a venture. Toscanelli replied enthusiastically. Not only did he give Columbus precise sailing directions, but he enclosed a chart that he had drawn up of the Atlantic Ocean. He estimated the distance between Lisbon and Japan as slightly more than 3,000 nautical miles. On the basis of his own calculations, Columbus reduced this mileage figure to 2,500. It is a good thing Columbus didn't know that the actual beeline distance between Europe and

32

Japan is more than 10,000 miles, for even his stout heart would probably have sunk at the thought of such a preposterous voyage over an unknown sea.

WHO STOLE COLUMBUS' CHARTS?

But confidence in getting to the Far East by sailing west was one thing. Rounding up the ships, men,

Paul the Physicist

The King of Portugal plotted to steal Columbus' chart.

and money for the venture was quite another. First, Columbus went to King John II of Portugal. King John was an adventurer by nature, and Columbus' daring ideas appealed to him. In spite of the objections of some of his advisors, it is likely that the King might have financed the expedition if Columbus had not made such exorbitant demands for himself. Not only did he want a large share of any treasure that he might find, but he also demanded titles and honors far beyond any that the King felt he could bestow on a common Italian sea captain.

That did not mean that John II lost all interest in the scheme, however. He asked Columbus to give him a copy of his charts and sailing plans so that he could study them while he made up his mind. He then turned them over to one of his own captains with instructions to sail westward to Cathay.

The captain duly started out; but when he had gone a few miles from land, with nothing ahead of him but the dreaded Sea of Darkness, he lost his courage and started back to Lisbon. The excuse that he gave the King for his quick return is not recorded. If he had gone on, it might well be that we would now celebrate "Somebody-or-Other-Day," instead of Columbus Day, every year.

When Columbus heard about this shabby trick, he left Lisbon in a fury and went to the Court of Ferdinand and Isabella in Spain.

WHO FINANCED COLUMBUS?

The Spaniards were involved at that time in a war to drive the last of the Moors out of southern Spain, and the King and Queen had little time to think about overseas adventure. Once more, Columbus and his great dream were shunted to one side. While

34

Queen Isabella at last agreed to finance Columbus' voyage.

he waited at the Spanish Court, he sent his brother Bartholomew to London to try to interest King Henry VII in the venture, and also to France to talk to King Charles VIII. Neither the English nor the French King was willing to put up the necessary money.

Meanwhile, Columbus hung on in Spain, clinging to a slim thread of hope that Queen Isabella, the real ruler of Spain, still held out to him. Then, like a bolt out of the sky, his dream started to come true. Persuaded by the royal treasurer, Isabella agreed to finance the voyage soon after the Moors had finally been defeated and chased back into Africa. This great event had happened at last on January 2, 1492, with the surrender of the Moorish capital of Granada. Now, Isabella was free to turn her attention to the business of finding a sea route to the East.

But again, as he had at the Court of King John in Portugal, Columbus almost lost Court backing by his extravagant personal demands. He insisted that he be named Admiral of the Ocean Sea, and appointed viceroy of all lands that he might discover. He also demanded one-eighth of all the profits from the venture. At first, Isabella refused; then, on a sudden impulse, she changed

Columbus promised his share of profits from the voyage to help free Jerusalem from Turkish tyranny.

her mind and agreed to give him her support. Now, with his lifelong ambition within grasp, Columbus vowed to devote his share of the profits to freeing the Holy City of Jerusalem from the infidel Turks.

In the little town of Palos, Columbus found three small vessels which were to go down in history — the Niña, the Pinta, and the Santa María. The next problem

Columbus first set sail from Palos, a small port in south-western Spain.

was to enlist crews, for even the hardy seafaring folk of Palos had no appetite for a long voyage across the dreaded Sea of Darkness into the unknown.

Columbus arranged to have criminals released from jail if they would serve as crew; he managed to have the debts of other men forgiven on the same condition. He offered all hands a liberal share in any treasure that might be found. One by one, he got together a crew of about 90 men, plus a captain for each ship.

36

So at dawn on Friday, August 3, 1492, the little fleet upped anchor and set a course for the Canary Islands, a Spanish possession off the coast of Africa. From there, Columbus planned to sail due west to Cipangu.

Bad luck struck on the third day out. The Pinta's rudder broke. But the captain, Martin Pinzon, managed to limp his ship into the Canaries and make repairs. After spending five weeks in the islands, Columbus again

The Niña, the Pinta, and the Santa María cross the dreaded Sea of Darkness.

headed his tiny armada into the setting sun. Now, nothing stood between him and Cipangu but the Sea of Darkness.

WHY WAS THE CREW FRIGHTENED?

To the ignorant sailors, the Sea of Darkness was a fearsome place. Legend said that it was guarded by horrible monsters which would destroy any ship that

37

ventured into it. Most people, including Columbus'
crew, believed that the earth was flat, and that when
they came to the outermost edge of the sea, they would
fall off into some eerie and fiery limbo. The wonder is
that any of the crew, except the captains, had agreed
to come along on the voyage in the first place.

Then, on September 16, after sailing 800 miles
from the Canaries, the men's worst fears were realized.
The ships sailed into the Sargasso Sea, a vast area of
almost solid seaweed which lies northeast of the Caribbean. As far as the eye could see, the surface of the
water looked like a floating meadow. At night, the phos-
phorescent light of the countless billions of microscopic
plants and protozoans with which the Sargasso abounds
threw off an eerie glow that convinced the sailors that
the sea was on fire. A week of sailing before steady trade
winds, however, saw them through the "sea of grass,"
and they were in open water again. A spanking breeze
from the northeast pushed the little ships steadily forward under pleasant, sun-kissed skies.

Columbus sighted land
on October 10, 1492,
just as the crew was
demanding rebelliously
that he turn back.

Under any other circumstances, it would have turned into a pleasant trip. But the men were becoming frightened again. On October 10, a little more than one day away from landing, the crews rebelled and demanded that their Admiral turn back. Already, the log showed that they had sailed much farther than Columbus' original estimate of 2,500 miles. And by this time, Columbus himself was becoming worried. He feared that he might possibly have gone to the north of Cipangu and missed it altogether. But he succeeded in persuading his men to bear with him for just three more days. They sailed on.

The next morning brought signs of land. The men saw branches floating in the water, with leaves and berries on them, pieces of wood, a wooden cane that seemed to be hand-carved. Sandpipers and other shore birds flew out over the ships. Now, excitement ran high among the crewmen. All their fears of the past few days and weeks were forgotten. Surely, by the next day, they would see exotic Cipangu!

No one slept that night. The Queen had promised a rich reward to the first man to sight land, and the sailors lined the rails straining their eyes into the tropic darkness.

Then, at two o'clock that morning of October 12, a sailor standing in the foretop spotted a faint line of surf breaking on a long strip of moonlit beach. "Land! Land!" he shouted frantically. At dawn, with great excitement, the boats were lowered and Columbus, with a part of his company, rowed over the sparkling blue water and into the palm-lined beach. Columbus stepped ashore first, planted the flag of Ferdinand and Isabella in the sand, and claimed the land for Spain.

The men crowded around him, kissing his hands, kneeling at his feet, and begging his forgiveness for their lack of faith. Their hearts were bursting with joy and thanksgiving, for they were sure that all of them would soon be wealthy beyond their wildest dreams.

Columbus landed on what is now known as Watling Island, and planted the flag of Isabella and Ferdinand.

CHAPTER 5

THE NEW WORLD

IT WAS a beautiful land that Columbus had found, abounding in lush greenery and brilliant flowers. But for all of its loveliness, it was a wilderness. Where were the great cities of the Khan, the busy harbors, the palaces with roofs of gold? Since the air all around was fragrant with rich perfume, Columbus concluded that he had landed on one of the spice islands which Marco Polo had described. Although Columbus would never know, the spice islands lay 10,000 miles farther west.

WHERE DID COLUMBUS THINK HE WAS?

There is still some question about the exact island in the Bahamas that Columbus first discovered. Many historians believe that it was the small cay which is now called Watling Island. In any case, Columbus named it "San Salvador"; its real name, as spoken by the natives that he would presently meet, was "Guanahani." They emerged in small groups from the forest and gaped timidly at the strange foreigners. But instead of wearing fine robes of silk, they were naked, save for designs painted

41

on their skins. Since he was certain that he was somewhere in the Indies, Columbus called them "Indians," a name that has been used for all American aborigines ever since.

When they saw that the Spaniards were not going to harm them, the Indians came forward and knelt down before the white men, probably thinking that they were gods who had come from the sky. In a little

Believing he was in the Indies, Columbus named the natives Indians.

while, they became bold enough to trade such things as tame parrots and bits of cotton thread for beads, little bells, and other trinkets. A few of the natives wore tiny gold ornaments around their necks. When Columbus asked them, in crude sign language, where the gold had come from, they pointed south. South, then, must be the way to Cipangu.

Taking some of the Indians along as guides, Columbus turned southward. When, after several days, he sighted Cuba, he thought that this surely must be Cipangu at last. His spirits brightened. He decided to spend a week or two in that country, trading for gold and spices, perhaps, and learning all he could about its arts and commerce. Then, a short, easy sail across would bring him to Cathay, where he would deliver the letter of greeting which the Spanish monarchs had written to the Great Khan.

WHY DID COLUMBUS DECIDE TO LEAVE?

But instead of the splendors of Japan, all that he found on Cuba were native villages surrounded by

fields of cotton, and such unknown vegetables as corn and potatoes. The Indians smoked a strange weed, tobacco, rolled in the shape of cigars. As the English settlers in Virginia would discover a little more than a century later, tobacco was to prove more valuable than all the spices of the Orient.

For the next three months, Columbus sailed around the islands of the Caribbean, searching for signs of gold and spices, and greatly puzzled because there were none. Then, on a reef near the present Cape Haitien in the Republic of Haiti, disaster struck a hard blow. His largest ship, the Santa María, ran up on a hidden reef and was pounded to pieces by the surf. Fearful that the same sort of accident might happen to his remaining two ships, Columbus determined to return to Spain at once, report on the strange lands that he had found beyond the Sea of Darkness, and secure more men and ships for a second voyage. With the experience of this first venture, he would surely find his way through the islands to Cipangu and Cathay on his next trip.

But now there was the problem of the men. With the Santa María gone, there was not room for all of them in the remaining two boats. The men themselves solved this difficulty. The islands were lovelier than any land they had ever seen before. The natives seemed friendly. Food abounded. And there was always the prospect that gold was near at hand. So 40 of them agreed to stay behind. They built huts from the timbers of the wrecked ship, and called their new colony "La Navidad."

(When Columbus visited the colony the next year, it had been wiped out by the Indians. All that was left of the 40 men were a few skeletons.)

Sailing west from Spain before the trade winds had been easy going. Getting back was a different thing. South of the Azores, the little ships ran into a howling Atlantic storm and they were battered unmerci-

Columbus returned to Spain, not with the gold and spices he had promised, but with parrots and painted Indians.

fully. Expecting to be sunk by the towering waves, Columbus wrote out an account of his voyage, which he sealed in wax, put into a watertight barrel, and threw overboard. He hoped that it might somehow wash up on shore and let the world know what had become of him. In the fury of the winds and waves, the Niña and Pinta were separated. But on March 15th, 1493, 224 days after they had started from this same port, both caravels limped into the harbor of Palos within hours of each other.

Columbus' return to Spain was a triumph for him. The parrots and painted Indians that he brought back with him were sensations. At the Royal Court in Barcelona, the King and Queen received him with highest honors. Although he had found no treasure except a few insignificant gold trinkets and a handful of doubtful pearls which his men had picked up in Cuba, it was obvious that he had made a great discovery. Surely, Cuba was an extremity of either Cipangu or Cathay. It stood to reason, too, that the great Admiral could easily make his way to the storied treasure cities on his next try. Ferdinand and Isabella dipped happily into the Spanish treasury to finance his second voyage, dreaming of the riches that he would certainly bring back to them. Now that the dreaded Sea of Darkness

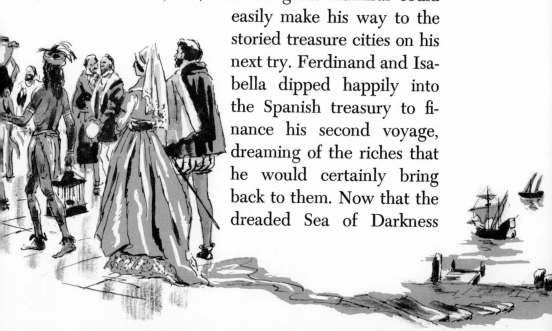

was no longer dark nor fearsome, young adventurers fought for the privilege of going along as common seamen and soldiers.

WHAT HAPPENED ON COLUMBUS' SECOND VOYAGE?

So it was that, on September 25, 1493, Columbus set out on his second voyage to the New World. This time, he had 17 fine ships and 1,500 men.

Although the second voyage started out from Spain in a blaze of glory, it did no more to swell the treasury of the Spanish King and Queen than had the first one. Columbus was still looking for Cathay; he was sure that he was very close to it.

For three years, his fleet wandered among the islands. They discovered Guadaloupe, Antigua, Haiti, Jamaica, and Puerto Rico. On these islands, they found Indians much fiercer than any they had met before. These Indians killed some of Columbus' men with poisoned arrows, and ate human flesh which they first smoked like hams. They were called the "Canibales"; from them, we get the word "cannibal."

Columbus built a headquarters city near the site of the original colony that had been wiped out by the Indians. Now, ships could come from Spain with supplies. But even though the first feeble settlement of the New World was beginning, Columbus persisted in the belief that he had found the eastern coast of Asia, and kept looking vainly for Cathay.

Twice more, Columbus made voyages to the world he had accidentally discovered. In the course of these expeditions, he explored the coasts of Central America, Panama, and South America. Through it all, he could never understand why Cipangu and Cathay were not where the maps of Paul the Physicist had said they should be. At last, in November, 1504, he returned to Spain for the last time — still firmly believing that he had found Asia. It never once occurred to him that he would go down in history.

The tragedy of Christopher Columbus is that he died in poverty and disgrace. Why? He had claimed that he would open up a rich trade route to the Orient. He had, in fact, opened up a whole new world, but that was not important at the time. No one realized the greatness of his discovery. To himself, his King and Queen, Columbus was a failure. They had little use for him once they realized he could not swell the Spanish treasury. They even took back the titles and honors they had given him.

Many great men have died unhailed and unsung by their own generations. Columbus was one of these men. The death of the Admiral on May 21, 1506, passed unnoticed. No chronicler of his time even mentioned it.

It is ironic that the great Western Hemisphere which he had stumbled upon — comprising half the

Columbus spent three years searching among the islands for Cathay.

world — was not named for Columbus, but for a minor explorer whose name would otherwise mean nothing to us.

WHY WAS THE NEW WORLD NAMED AMERICA?

Amerigo Vespucci was an astronomer and geographer who made several trips to South America. The vastness of the land, its high mountains, and the broad rivers flowing down out of them, convinced him that, instead of being a part of Asia, this was indeed a new and unknown continent. On his return to Europe, he wrote letters to several geographers suggesting this possibility.

One of these letters found its way to a young German map-maker named Martin Waldseemuller. When, in 1507, Waldseemuller published a new book of geography, he first outlined the three known parts of the world — Europe, Asia, and Africa. Then, he added a fourth.

"I see no reason," he wrote, "why we should not call this new world after its discoverer, Amerigo."

And across this part of his map, he inscribed the name, "America."

The new continent is added to the map.

CHAPTER 6

CABOT FINDS NORTH AMERICA

GIOVANNI CABOTO, like Columbus, was a native of Genoa, Italy. He, too, was a skilled map-maker and navigator, and had independently worked out a plan for getting to the Indies by going west. Because he sailed under the English flag, he had changed his name to John Cabot.

Years before Columbus' first voyage, Cabot had been involved in the spice trade with the Near East. When he asked where these spices had come from, the Moslem traders replied that they had been brought great distances, by a succession of camel caravans, from an Asian land that lay to the east and north. Thus, Cabot got the idea — at about the same time Columbus did — of reaching the Orient by sailing due west from England.

At first, he could find no support for this unheard-of scheme. But when news reached London that Columbus had successfully completed such a voyage on behalf of the King of Spain, King Henry VII quickly gave Cabot his royal permission to try to do the same thing for England.

49

John Cabot discovered New-foundland. Nearby, he found the waters teeming with fish. They were the now-famous Newfoundland Banks.

WHERE DID JOHN CABOT LAND?

Financed by the merchants of Bristol, who did not relish the prospect of a Spanish empire, Cabot sailed from that port in May of 1947. On June 24, he sighted the coast of the large mass of land he named "New Found Land." He went ashore just long enough to plant the English flag and thus claim the country for King Henry. He found a few animal snares and bone tools, which convinced him that the land was inhabited.

More important, he found that the waters off-shore were teeming with vast schools of fish, so thick that they could be dipped out of the water with baskets. This was the famous Newfoundland Banks, still the world's most fertile fishing grounds. Having observed this much, Cabot hurried back to England to report that he had found the mainland of Asia.

John Cabot was the first white man, since the vikings, to set foot on the mainland of North America.

50

The next year, Cabot sailed west again. This time, he had a number of ships, all loaded with the kind of trade goods that Marco Polo had said would be best for trading with the merchants of Cathay. There would be plenty of cargo space on the return voyage for the riches that Cabot planned to bring back from the land of the Khan. He also took along his son, Sebastian.

WHO WAS SEBASTIAN CABOT?

The old records do not reveal anything more about John Cabot after his departure on this second voyage. Unlike Columbus, he kept no careful logs of his voyage. We do know, however, that it was a tragic, unfulfilled venture and that he died in obscurity shortly after his return to England.

At any rate, it was Sebastian who claimed credit for his father's discoveries — but he wove such a tangled skein of lies that, to this day, nobody has been able to cut through it to find the real truth of what happened.

As nearly as we can come to putting the events of this second voyage together, Cabot first cruised along the coast of Greenland. Then his small fleet turned south, past Newfoundland, and down the coasts of New England. It is possible that Cabot and his men even went

as far as Florida. All the while, they kept looking for signs of Cathay. But they saw nothing except towering forests that stretched endlessly toward the west.

Finally, in the fall, Cabot's ships gave up and sailed back to England, their holds still filled with the useless trade goods. The Bristol merchants resolved to put up no more money for such foolish ventures in the future. King Henry was disgusted, and promptly lost interest in any lands that might lie westward. It was not until more than half a century later that a British ruler, Queen Elizabeth, sent her sea-dogs across the Atlantic to the New World.

WERE THE SPANISH EXPLORERS SUCCESSFUL?

Meanwhile, the Spaniards had staked out America as their own private property. They found pearls in great quantity and vast amounts of gold. But, what is more important, in their endless search for treasure, they explored a whole new land — furthering the discovery of America that Columbus had begun.

Ponce de Leon discovered the Florida mainland in 1513.

Juan de Urijalva discovered the Aztec Empire in 1518.

Aztec fire god.

Hernando de Soto crossed the great Mississippi in 1540.

Vasco Núñez de Balboa climbed a mountain on the narrow neck of Panama and saw the Pacific Ocean from the west for the first time. Wading out into its gentle surf, he claimed it — and all the lands bordering on it—for the King of Spain.

Juan Ponce de León, looking for gold and a legendary fountain of youth, discovered the mainland of Florida in 1513.

Sailing along the west coast of Florida a few years later, Alonzo Alvarez de Pineda found the mouth of the Mississippi. In 1540, Hernando De Soto crossed the great river itself.

Balboa climbed a mountain on the narrow neck of Panama, and discovered the Pacific Ocean in 1513. He claimed all the surrounding land for Spain.

Juan de Urijalva sailed from Cuba across the Caribbean to Mexico, and there discovered the fabulous empire of the Aztecs, the first true treasure trove that was found in the New World.

In 1519, Hernando Cortes invaded the Aztecs of Mexico, took their Emperor Montezuma prisoner, and looted the land of tons of gold which he sent back to Spain.

Later, Francisco Pizarro sailed south from Panama and discovered the empire of the Incas in Peru. (From it, he took gold and jewels estimated at well over $100 million.) In so doing, he opened up the western coast of South America for exploration.

Then, in the last of the great Spanish exploratory expeditions, a young aristocrat named Francisco Vasquez de Coronado probed into the vast heartland of what is now the United States by approaching it, for a change, from the west.

Cortes undertook the conquest of Mexico in 1519, and, after fierce fighting, defeated the Aztecs.

CHAPTER 7

THE SEVEN GOLDEN CITIES

A TALE was told in "New Spain," as the Spanish conquerors had renamed Mexico, about seven fantastic cities that lay somewhere to the north. The legend said gold was so plentiful in these cities that the people used it to make ordinary tools. Precious jewels were rumored to be as common as pebbles, and to be picked up in the streets. In their greed for the wealth of the New World, the Spaniards were ready to believe anything. And so, in the year 1540, the Governor of "New Spain" sent an army under Coronado to go forth, find these cities, and bring back their treasures.

With a force of some 300 armored horsemen, and a large number of foot soldiers, Indian allies among them, Coronado crossed the high deserts of northern Mexico and passed into what is now Arizona. Here, he found his first city, but it was only a miserable town of mud huts inhabited by belligerent Zuni Indians. After bitter battle, Coronado and his men moved on, tired, dirty, and discouraged.

55

They crossed New Mexico, just as dry and dismal as Arizona, and went on into Texas. But there were no cities, and no gold. Nothing but cactus and rattlesnakes.

Seeking the Seven Cities, Coronado led his men from Mexico into Arizona, and then farther north. They were the first white men to see the Grand Canyon.

Some of the soldiers tried to pick up these odd creatures, whose tails made such a musical sound, and were bitten to death for their trouble.

Coronado was a stubborn man, and he kept going on in search of the golden cities. He saw herds of buffaloes, curious beasts to the Spaniards, that covered the rolling plains by the millions, like a huge, brown moving carpet. His soldiers were the first white men to see the glories of the Grand Canyon and to see the pueblos of the prehistoric cliff dwellers. But still there was no sign of the fabled Seven Cities.

56

At last, Coronado was about ready to turn back to Mexico when an Indian came into camp with a story that sent the young Spaniard's hopes soaring once again. He knew, the Indian said, the location of the Seven Cities. If the white men would only follow him, he would lead the way to them.

WHO WAS THE TURK?

This Indian — Coronado's men called him the Turk because he wore a cloth turban on his head — then proceeded to take the army on one of history's most fantastic wild goose chases. He led them through the hills and badlands of Oklahoma, up across the great grasslands of Kansas, and into the very middle of what is now America.

An Indian called the Turk promised to lead Coronado to the Seven Cities.

They saw the Plains Indians living in their tepee villages — the Kiowa, Comanche, Arapaho, and Sioux. They saw the broad prairies that would, one day, blossom with waving fields of corn and wheat. But they saw not one golden city, nor even one nugget of gold.

After many months of marching, Coronado was forced to the conclusion that he had been the victim of a hoax. When he confronted the Turk, the Indian admitted that he had deliberately led the Spaniards astray so that their horses would weaken and the men would be stranded to die of starvation on the empty plains. Coronado's soldiers killed the Turk on the spot, and then they began their dreary retreat of something like 2,000 miles back to Mexico City, which they had left in such high spirits more than two years before.

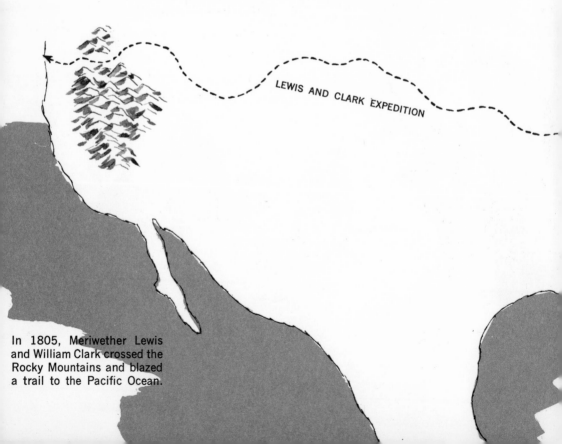

In 1805, Meriwether Lewis and William Clark crossed the Rocky Mountains and blazed a trail to the Pacific Ocean.

So ended the first exploration of the interior of America. But this was only the beginning.

In 1682, a young Frenchman named René Robert Cavelier de la Salle journeyed from Canada, through the Great Lakes, and down the Mississippi to the Gulf of Mexico.

A century later, Daniel Boone left the seacoast colonies and found the vast lands of Kentucky and Tennessee that lay beyond the western mountains.

Meriwether Lewis and William Clark, in 1805, struck west from the Missouri, crossed the Rocky Mountains, and blazed the overland trail to the Pacific Ocean.

At last, the discovery of America — the great adventure that had begun more than 300 years before

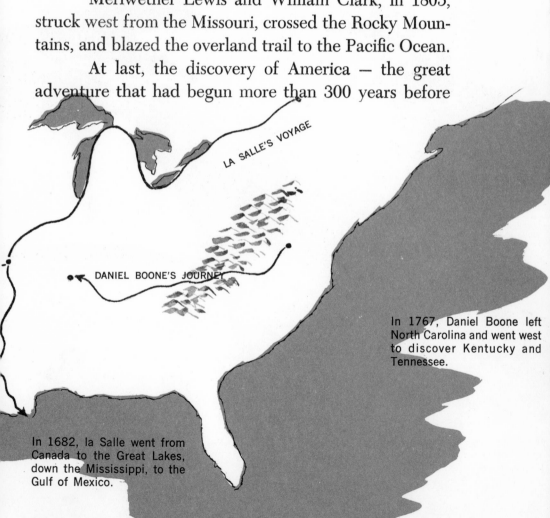

In 1767, Daniel Boone left North Carolina and went west to discover Kentucky and Tennessee.

In 1682, la Salle went from Canada to the Great Lakes, down the Mississippi, to the Gulf of Mexico.

when a sailor standing in the foretop of the Santa María saw the surf-sprayed beaches of a moonlit island in the middle of a Sea of Darkness — was completed.

INDEX